Wedges

by Anne Welsbacher

Consultant:
Philip W. Hammer, Ph.D.
Assistant Manager of Education
American Institute of Physics

Bridgestone Books
an imprint of Capstone Press
Mankato, Minnesota

Bridgestone Books are published by Capstone Press
151 Good Counsel Drive, P.O. Box 669, Mankato, Minnesota 56002
http://www.capstone-press.com

Library of Congress Cataloging-in-Publication Data
Welsbacher, Anne, 1955–.
    Wedges/by Anne Welsbacher.
    p. cm.—(The Bridgestone Science Library)
    Includes bibliographical references and index.
    Summary: Uses everyday examples to show how wedges are simple machines that
make pushing, pulling apart, and lifting easier.
    ISBN 0-7368-0614-8
    1. Wedges—Juvenile literature. [1. Wedges.] I. Title. II. Series.
TJ 1201.W44 W45 2001
621.8'11—dc21
                                                              00-023989

Editorial Credits
Rebecca Glaser, editor; Linda Clavel, cover designer; Kia Bielke, illustrator; Katy Kudela,
    photo researcher

Photo Credits
David F. Clobes, 14, 16
Jack Glisson, 8
Kimberly Danger, cover, 4, 10, 18
Unicorn Stock Photos/Jeff Greenberg, 12
Visuals Unlimited/Les Christman, 20

1 2 3 4 5 6 06 05 04 03 02 01

Table of Contents

Simple Machines. 5

Parts of a Wedge 7

Using Wedges to Cut 9

Using Wedges to Split. 11

Using Wedges to Push Apart 13

Using Wedges to Push Together 15

Using Wedges to Hold Tight 17

Using Wedges to Grip. 19

Wedges in Complex Machines. 21

Hands On: Cutting with Wedges. 22

Words to Know 23

Read More 24

Internet Sites 24

Index. 24

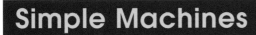

Simple Machines

Simple machines make work easier or faster. Work is using force to move an object across a distance. Cutting, splitting, and pushing are kinds of work. Wedges are simple machines that people use to cut, split, or push.

force

anything that changes the speed, direction, or motion of an object

5

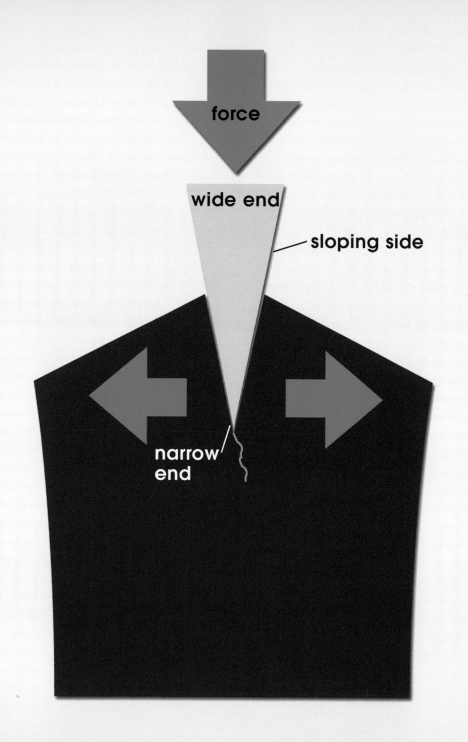

Parts of a Wedge

A wedge has a wide end and a narrow end. A wedge has one or two sloping sides. Force on the wedge's wide end makes the narrow end go into an object. The narrow end makes a path for the thicker end. The wedge splits the object.

Using Wedges to Cut

Most cutting tools have wedges. A knife blade is a wedge. The knife's narrow edge slides easily into food. Scissor blades are wedges. The sharp wedge-shaped edges allow scissors to cut through paper or cloth.

Using Wedges to Split

Wedges help split objects. An ax is a wedge that people use to split wood. Teeth are wedges that help people bite into foods. The thin edge of a tooth enters a carrot. The tooth then pushes deeper to break off a piece of the carrot.

Using Wedges to Push Apart

A wedge pushes things apart. A boat's bow is a wedge. The bow's wedge shape pushes water away from the boat. The blade of a plow is a wedge. A plow blade pushes dirt to make rows for planting.

bow
the front end of a boat

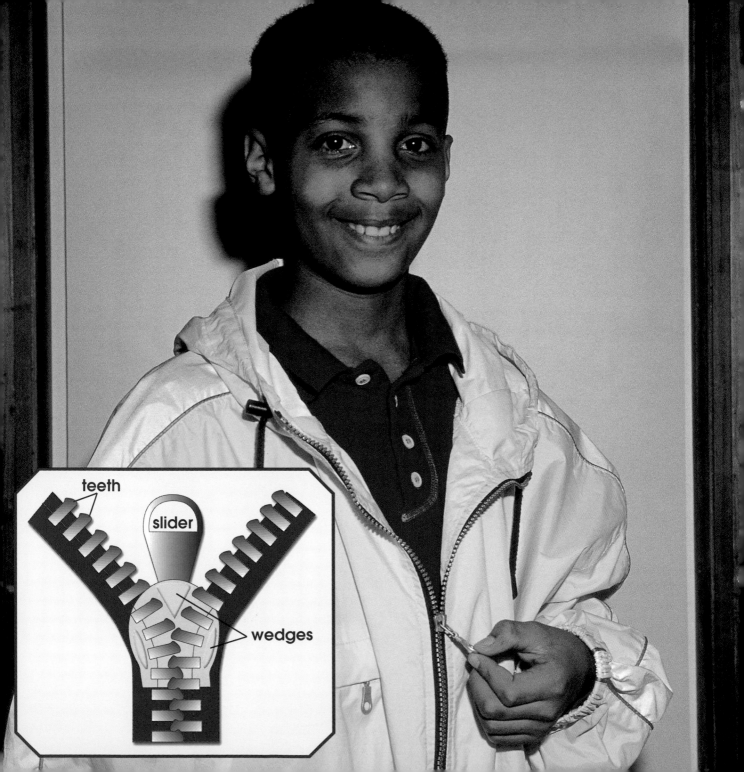

teeth

slider

wedges

Using Wedges to Push Together

Wedges can push things together. Zippers use wedges. Wedges inside the slider push the zipper teeth together. Each zipper tooth also is a wedge. The wedges fit into each other and hold tight.

Using Wedges to Hold Tight

The sloping side of a wedge is an inclined plane. The inclined plane helps a wedge hold objects in place. A doorstop holds a door open. The thin end of a doorstop fits under the door. The inclined plane pushes up against the bottom of the door.

inclined plane
a flat surface that slants; an inclined plane is a simple machine.

17

Using Wedges to Grip

Wedges can hold objects together. The tip of a nail is a wedge. The wedge shape helps the nail slide into wood easily. Nails hold boards together. Push pins also have wedge-shaped tips. A push pin holds paper on a bulletin board.

Wedges in Complex Machines

Simple machines are part of complex machines. A bulldozer is a complex machine that moves dirt. The blade of a bulldozer is a wedge. The blade cuts into dirt. The bulldozer scoops the dirt and pushes it away.

complex
having many parts

21

Hands On: Cutting with Wedges

This activity will show you how a wedge shape makes cutting easier. You can make your own play dough and cut shapes.

What You Need

1 1/2 cups (375 mL) flour   3/4 cup (175 mL) salt
3/4 cup (175 mL) water   Food coloring
Mixing bowl   Wooden spoon
Plastic knife   Airtight container or plastic bag

What You Do

1. Mix the flour, salt, water, and food coloring together in a bowl with the wooden spoon.
2. Wet your fingers. Finish mixing the dough with your hands.
3. Roll part of the dough into a ball.
4. Try to cut the ball in half with the flat side of the knife.
5. Now try cutting the dough with the sharp edge of the knife. The wedge shape makes cutting easier.
6. Use the knife to cut and create other shapes or figures.
7. Store your dough in an airtight container or plastic bag so you can use it again.

Wedges such as knives make cutting easier. The knife's narrow end makes a path for the wide end.

Words to Know

bow (BOU)—the front end of a boat

force (FORSS)—anything that changes the speed, direction, or motion of an object

inclined plane (in-KLINDE PLANE)—a flat surface that slants; an inclined plane is a simple machine.

work (WURK)—using force to move an object across a distance

Read More

Armentrout, Patricia. *The Wedge.* Simple Devices. Vero Beach, Fla.: Rourke, 1997.

Glover, David. *Ramps and Wedges.* Simple Machines. Crystal Lake, Ill.: Rigby Interactive Library, 1997.

Hodge, Deborah. *Simple Machines.* Starting with Science. Toronto: Kids Can Press, 1996.

Internet Sites

Inventors Toolbox: Simple Machines
http://www.mos.org/sln/Leonardo/InventorsToolbox.html

School Zone, Simple Machines
http://www.science-tech.nmstc.ca/maindex.cfm?idx=1394&language=english&museum=sat&function=link&pidx=1394

Simple Machines
http://www.fi.edu/qa97/spotlight3/spotlight3.html

Index

ax, 11
blade, 9, 13, 21
bulldozer, 21
complex machine, 21
doorstop, 17
force, 5, 7
inclined plane, 17
nail, 19
simple machine, 5, 21
tooth, 11, 15
work, 5
zipper, 15